# The 4 Elements

Text: **Núria Roca**

Illustrations: **Rosa M. Curto**

**BARRON'S**

Close your eyes and imagine the planet where you live with your family and your friends and aaaaall the rest of the people in the world. Also imagine all the animals, and flowers, and even tiny forms of life called microbes. You live on a **planet** with air that ruffles your hair, water that gets you wet, fire that keeps you warm, and the earth that allows all kinds of plants and trees to grow.

**Guess** what it is: You can't touch it or see it but it is all around. When it is still, you don't realize it is there, but when it moves, it shakes the leaves on the trees, whistles in your ears, and makes the clothes you are wearing begin to dance. Sometimes it **blows** so hard it seems it doesn't let you walk. Did you guess? It's the air!

Breathe in air through your nose and then blow it out of your mouth. Can you notice how your lungs become filled with air and then get empty? People need the oxygen in the air to be able to **breathe.** That's why we can't stay long under the water.

If you were a shark or other fish, what would you need to breathe in the water? Gills! A fish's gills can take air out of the water and then the fish can breathe.

**Air** is strong enough to hold birds up in the sky as well as planes, kites, air balloons ... and a lot more things! It is so **strong** it can turn the blades of a windmill to create electricity!

Sometimes we forget how important air is, and we pollute it with car exhaust and factory fumes. But we all need clean air! **Can you** name everything you see on the opposite page?